THE SECRETS OF THE
SITH

BY MARC SUMERAK

ILLUSTRATIONS BY SERGIO GÓMEZ SILVÁN

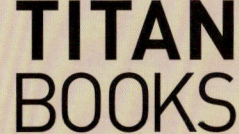

London, United Kingdom

INTRODUCTION

The Sith Order lives!

The rebel fools believed I could be killed. That the ways of the Sith would die along with me. So I let them cling to hope, like the pathetic creatures they are, desperately grasping for the light, just beyond their reach.

But darkness is eternal. Unlike the light, it cannot be extinguished. It will always find a way to rise again. And I, Darth Sidious, have risen with it.

My old Empire crumbled, undone by the weakness and betrayal of those beneath me. Yet those who worshipped the Sith—who exalted the dark side of the Force—lived on. In the shadows of the Unknown Regions, they grew ever stronger. In my name, they prepared to strike back. To vanquish those who sought to end my reign. To unleash my righteous vengeance.

THE CODE OF THE SITH

These loyal followers, my Sith Eternal, carried out my grand scheme, ensuring my return. Not merely my return to life—my return to total supremacy! For a Sith Lord craves absolute power, and nothing will stop me from attaining it. Not even death itself.

Yet such power takes time to amass. As always, my plans were infallible, but they could not be rushed. To ensure my efforts would bear fruit, every eventuality was considered. Every move carefully calculated. Failure was not an option.

For decades, my endeavors have been performed in secret. From the forgotten Sith planet of Exegol, I stoked conflict in the New Republic. As the galaxy spiraled into turmoil once more, my plot was set in motion—the restoration of the Sith and the reclamation of my throne. As light began to fade across all systems, the day of my ascension drew ever closer.

That day has finally come.

After years of preparation, my plans have reached their final stage. As my Final Order prepares to rise, news of my return shall echo across the galaxy. From beyond the grave, my voice shall be broadcast for all to hear. Those who believed that I could be destroyed will be shown their greatest mistake.

At last the work of generations is complete. The great error is corrected. The day of victory is at hand. The day of revenge.

The day of the Sith.

THE DARK SIDE

Throughout my existence, I have built Empires and decimated planets. Yet no power I have held compares with that of the dark side of the Force. This limitless field of cosmic energy flows through us all. It feeds off our passion and makes our darkest desires a reality. For one such as I, the dark side offers unlimited power. Harness its full fury, and all things are possible.

OPPOSING FORCES

Feeble minds have struggled to comprehend the Force's vast potential for millennia, studying its two aspects—the light side and the dark side. The weak sought to limit themselves to the light. They shunned the dark side, believing it to be a path to corruption. But the brightest of lights casts the darkest of shadows. That darkness must be allowed to bleed through. For only those who choose to embrace the dark side are able to truly exploit the boundless potential of the Force.

FEAR, ANGER, HATE, SUFFERING

The dark side of the Force is fueled by raw emotion. Naive fools who devote themselves solely to the light believe that passion obscures judgment. But those who embrace the dark side see far more clearly. We find strength in our fury. Terror, pain, and rage become our greatest tools. Our passion is our power, and that power should never be underestimated. But while the dark side gives, so it takes. It hungers like a flame that must be fed. Those who master its ways will be unstoppable. Those who cannot will be consumed.

THE JEDI ORDER

Worshipping only the light, the Jedi appointed themselves guardians of so-called peace. Their Knights and masters spread their narrow view of the Force across the galaxy. In doing so, they poisoned the minds of all those they claimed to serve. The Jedi imagined the light would keep them pure, when in truth it made them blind. As their influence grew, so grew their arrogance. Convinced their path was the only answer, their imbecilic Order lost all sight of the darkness growing around them. Their minds clouded, the Jedi would become easy prey for their most ancient enemy.

THE SITH ORDER

Legend has it the Jedi Order suffered a deep schism millennia ago. An opposing sect dedicated to the glory of the dark side arose from the ashes. The Sith did not share the Jedi's myopic view of the Force. They embraced the dark side as a means to personal gain and ultimate victory. And, for a time, that great victory would be achieved. The Sith Order grew, spreading its might across the galaxy. But the Jedi became jealous. They would not tolerate a challenge to their authority. After thousands of years of war, the Sith were pushed to the edge of extinction. From the darkness, those who survived laid the foundations for our Order's return . . . and my rise to power.

REVENGE OF THE SITH

With the Sith forced into exile, the corrupt Jedi secured their foothold of power in the galaxy. They traveled to distant worlds, indoctrinating the masses while enforcing the laws of the Galactic Republic. With none to oppose them, their misguided Order reached its greatest heights. Thus, their inevitable fall would be all the more satisfying to behold.

OUT OF THE DARKNESS

After centuries in the shadows, the Sith were poised to emerge once more. As a dark apprentice, I sensed that the Galactic Republic was in disarray. Its delegates held no interest in the common good. They would be easy targets for my influence. Serving as a senator, I manipulated their greed in my favor. With each new act of legislation, I rose through their ranks. Total control of the galaxy's governing body drew ever closer. But ascension in the Senate would not be enough. My master, Darth Plagueis, had served his purpose. I struck him down, claiming his place as the one true master of the Sith. Under my rule, our Order would return to its rightful glory.

UNLIMITED POWER

Orchestrating a conflict on my homeworld of Naboo, I sowed the seeds of civil unrest. Chaos erupted within the Senate—a chaos I controlled on every front. When the crisis abated, I took control of the Senate, exactly as planned. As Supreme Chancellor Sheev Palpatine, I would stand for a united Republic. As Sith Lord Darth Sidious, I would conspire to rip that Republic asunder. My machinations led to the formation of a Separatist movement strong enough to upend the galactic status quo. With war on the horizon, the Senate granted me absolute authority without a moment's hesitation. My power, both in the Republic and in the dark side, would prove critical in bringing a young Jedi named Anakin Skywalker—a boy whose power nearly rivaled my own—under my thrall.

THE CLONE WARS

The Jedi Order would not be able to face the Separatists' massive droid army alone—of this I made certain. How fortunate, then, that I had been secretly directing the creation of a grand army of genetic duplicates obedient to my every command. For years, the Clone Wars raged across hundreds of worlds. The Jedi led their seemingly faithful clone troops in an onslaught of harrowing battles, their Order growing ever weaker. One last hope for victory remained: the capture of Separatist leader Count Dooku. But the Jedi and the Republic alike were too blind to see the truth. Dooku had been answering to me all along. As my Sith apprentice Darth Tyranus, Dooku had served me well. But unbeknownst even to him, his demise had always been a critical part of my plan. He fell by my command, struck down by my young ally, Skywalker. With the Separatist leader gone, the Clone Wars neared their conclusion. And my next apprentice took one step closer to the dark side.

DAWN OF THE EMPIRE

As my glorious war reached its climax, the covetous Jedi sought to overturn my control of the Republic. Incapable of seeing beyond the light, they vowed to take both my power and my life. Their craven attempt left me scarred and deformed, but their treachery was repaid in kind. Skywalker succumbed to the dark power I offered him and was reborn as my new apprentice, Darth Vader. The Jedi had been branded enemies of the Republic. Thus, the time had come to execute Order 66. This fail-safe—genetically programmed into every soldier in my vast army—compelled the clones to betray their generals, eliminating the fabled Jedi Order in an instant. The few Jedi who escaped their fate went into exile. The Republic was no more. The Galactic Empire rose in its place. And it belonged to the Sith.

THE JEDI RETURN

As Emperor, I reigned over the galaxy with unquestioned authority while Lord Vader administered my unrelenting justice. Any rebels misguided enough to stand in opposition to my rule were shown no mercy. Even when the accursed light of the Jedi sparked once more in the form of Vader's lost son, Luke Skywalker, I was prepared. I would turn the boy to the dark side, taking him as my new apprentice. But my efforts were cut short by the treachery of his father. As Vader hurled my body toward its inevitable demise, my great plan moved to its next phase. For my knowledge of the dark side was without equal. And its unlimited power was still with me . . .

UNNATURAL ABILITIES

The dark side of the Force is a pathway to many abilities some consider to be unnatural. Only through my unparalleled command of those uncanny practices was I able to survive certain death and rise again on Exegol. The unlimited might of the dark side restored my majesty. And now its infinite capacity for inducing suffering shall be unleashed upon the galaxy once more!

TRANSFERENCE

The Jedi accepted death as part of life. And so I gladly delivered that death to them. But the Sith are not content with the limitations of the physical realm. For centuries, our Order has seen the dark side of the Force as a means of achieving immortality. Yet none were able to unlock that secret . . . until Darth Plagueis the Wise. My master discovered ways to use the Force to keep others from perishing. But, alas, for all his infinite wisdom, he still could not save himself from death at the hand of his own trusted apprentice. I vowed that I would not make the same mistake. Studying his methods, I learned how to transfer my own consciousness, through the Force, from one mortal vessel to another. Even if my flesh was doomed to fail, my spirit would be eternal!

LIGHTNING

The abundant energies generated by the dark side can be made manifest, channeled into concentrated bursts of electricity capable of incalculable devastation. With this power, I have made the strongest of Jedi Masters beg for mercy. And I have shown them none. Even the greatest of Sith Lords is not immune to the destructive effects of this dark display.

PHYSICAL FORCE

The dark side of the Force can be utilized to cause great physical anguish. The Jedi squandered the Force, using it only for defense. But, for a disciple of the dark side, the Force is a weapon fueled by unbridled aggression. Through the dark side, foes can be lifted into the air, thrust against walls, or held in place to await their inexorable punishment. My former apprentice Lord Vader often used the Force to extend his mighty grip, crushing the throats of any who questioned his directives without ever laying a hand upon them. When unleashing the dark side, the possibilities are limitless.

TRICKS OF THE MIND

When one communes with the Force, they expand their consciousness on a galactic scale. Through the dark side, I have reached out across the void, finding a single mind in a sea of trillions. I have become the subtle voice in the minds of my victims, pushing them ever closer to the darkness. And I have forged bonds between individuals to push their fates toward each other in ways that would ultimately benefit my grand design. There are many who insist that the Force has spoken to them, but few realize that these whispers often emanate from the lips of a Sith Lord.

DARK LEGACY

With the Force as my guide, death would not be the final word in my story. But my fall would signal a necessary end to the Galactic Empire. If the vast and powerful forces I had gathered could not perform their sworn duty and protect their own Emperor, they did not deserve to lay claim to this galaxy in my absence. For their failures, I would see them burn. And the galaxy along with them.

CONTINGENCY

Resistance. Rebellion. Defiance. These foolish notions gained strength in my absence. They could not be allowed to persist. As such, posthumous directives were delivered to the Imperial fleet via automated Messengers bearing my likeness. Operation: Cinder was initiated, launching satellites to destroy key rebel planets as a final act of retribution. Soon, the remnants of my armada were united in one last battle above the planet Jakku, unaware that they were being sacrificed as penance for their negligence. With the Empire erased from existence, something new could rise in its place. And from beyond the grave, I would control its every move . . .

AN IMPERFECT SOLUTION

As the Empire perished, I was born again, my consciousness transferred into a new body on Exegol. Alas, even after years of experimentation, the cloning techniques employed by my acolytes were inadequate. They could not create a vessel capable of containing my unfathomable power. Though my soul remained complete, the flesh designed to house it began to fail. To continue my plans for total galactic domination, I would need a form worthy of my might. It was clear that this defective mortal shell would not be enough.

PULLING THE STRINGS

My new body's deformities were severe. Unable to leave Exegol, I would have to spread my influence across the galaxy through less direct means. As part of their genetic experiments, my followers had attempted to create another being that came to be known as Snoke. Although his body proved unworthy of containing my dark essence, Snoke's natural sensitivity to the Force would make him a powerful puppet nonetheless. Through my manipulation of Snoke, I began gathering forces, building an army capable of opposing the New Republic that had risen in my absence. Through Snoke, I would make certain that the First Order would be mine to control.

HEIR TO THE EMPIRE

Just as I shunned the inferior child spawned of my flesh, he shunned his "father" and the ways of the Sith. When he sired a genetic heir to my Empire, a new opportunity to ensure my legacy arose. But my errant clone and his mate absconded with their child and went into hiding. They were soon located on Jakku and dispatched for their betrayal. Yet their progeny—my granddaughter—remained safely hidden from my reach for many years. Until now. There has been an awakening—a young scavenger girl with the spirit of a true Jedi, yet filled with such pain and anger that she can barely resist the call to darkness. I have foreseen what she can become. For this young girl, known her whole life only as Rey, has more than just power. She has my power. And though she may fear who she truly is, I revel in that truth. She is a Palpatine. And soon, I shall make certain she embraces her destiny . . .

IN NAME ALONE

Snoke was a temporary measure at best. My faithful followers in the Unknown Regions still sought to produce a body worthy of my infinite might. Using a technique known as Strand-Casting, countless modified clone bodies were produced from my genetic template. All but one of them were utter failures. The lone subject that survived the cloning process lacked any connection to the Force. I rejected this useless creature, but I chose to let it live. Even if this "son" was undeserving of my legacy, I surmised that the Palpatine blood rushing through its veins might someday become useful. As always, my theory would soon prove correct . . .

THE CHOSEN ONE

None in this galaxy has ever proved my equal in the power of the dark side. But in matters of the Force, there is one bloodline that cannot be ignored—the Skywalkers. My most powerful apprentice, Darth Vader, was born a Skywalker. Though his darkness was feared across the galaxy, there remained a loathsome spark of light buried within him that he failed to smother.

BALANCE TO THE FORCE

Young Anakin Skywalker began life as nothing more than a slave on the desert world of Tatooine. But the boy was blessed with a power unrivaled by any except my own. Anakin was believed by the Jedi to be a vergence—an entity surrounded by a rare concentration of Force energy. They even convinced themselves that the child was the Chosen One, described in an ancient Jedi prophecy. So certain were they that Anakin would bring balance to the Force, they failed to consider what that might truly mean.

A GREAT FEAR

As Anakin's powers intensified, so did his emotions. He wanted more than his feckless Order could offer him. I planted seeds of doubt in his mind about the Jedi and their dogma. But it was not doubt that would lead young Skywalker to abandon the Jedi path—it was love, and the fear of losing it.

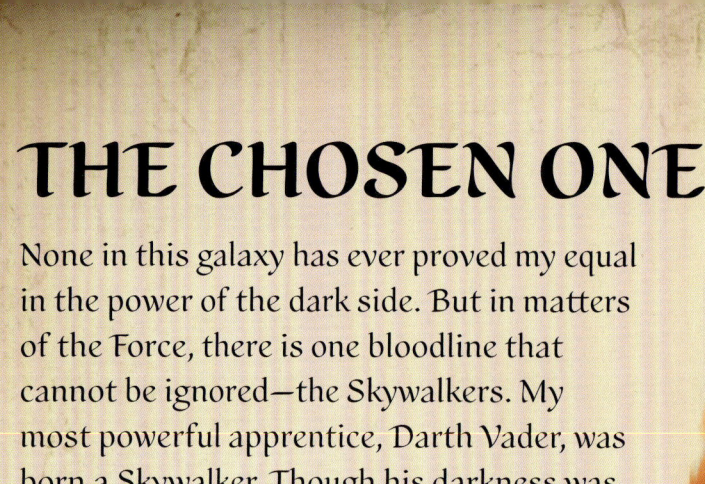

Though romantic entanglements were long forsaken by the Jedi, Anakin entered a forbidden union with a senator from Naboo named Padmé Amidala. Unsettling premonitions of his pregnant wife's demise troubled the boy. He was willing to do anything to prevent that future from unfolding. And I was there to offer him a solution.

DARK APPRENTICE

Revealing my true nature to young Skywalker, I presented the dark side as the only path to ensuring his beloved's survival. He submitted himself to me, a Jedi no longer, and rose as my new Sith apprentice, Darth Vader. At my command, he turned against the Jedi Order. He massacred his brethren at their own Temple, giving no quarter. He had returned balance to the Force indeed—by drowning out the light and freeing the darkness. But Lord Vader would have no time to revel in his triumph. Struck down by his former Jedi Master Obi-Wan Kenobi on Mustafar, he was left burned and mutilated. Though I managed to salvage his broken body and sustain his life, he would soon come to wish I had not.

AEON ENGINE

During his time on Mustafar, Lord Vader learned of a device designed to bridge the gap between life and death—the Aeon Engine. The cost of activating the Aeon Engine was steep, draining the life energies from Mustafar and those who dwelled there. But to obtain true dominion over death, any price is worth paying. The engine and the ancient crystal that powered it were destroyed before Vader could explore their full potential. But if such a device could be re-created, it would undoubtedly prove useful in the hands of the Sith.

FINAL BETRAYAL

Years later, Lord Vader found himself once again locked in combat with Obi-Wan Kenobi. My apprentice redeemed his past failure and struck down his former master. But he soon discovered that Kenobi had taken on a new apprentice—Luke Skywalker, a young boy strong in the Force whom Vader would soon learn was his own son. Lord Vader had believed his child had died with Padmé. It was the fear, pain, and suffering stemming from that loss that powered him for so long. But now a different emotion began to surface within him, one he had not experienced in ages—love. His fear of losing his wife had pushed him toward the dark side. To save his son, he would choose a different path. Lord Vader turned against the darkness and betrayed his true master. Anakin Skywalker was reborn, just in time to die, his pathetic display costing him his own life. And all for nothing. Vader was gone—but the Sith would return . . .

THE RISE AND FALL OF THE SKYWALKERS

The Skywalker legacy has long been tied to the Force through ancient prophecies and their bloodline's undeniable potential. My most powerful apprentice, Darth Vader, proved incapable of fulfilling his destiny with the dark side, but I have continued to watch the generations that followed him with great interest.

LUKE SKYWALKER

A self-appointed Jedi Master, the great Luke Skywalker wasted his life attempting to rebuild the fallen Jedi Order. That pathetic dream was shattered when Skywalker's prize pupil—his nephew, Ben Solo—turned against the Order's teachings and cut down his fellow students. Skywalker wallowed in self-pity, fleeing into seclusion and abandoning the ways of the Force. His exile allowed me to set in motion the plans for my return. Yet, if not for Luke Skywalker, perhaps none of my efforts would have been necessary. It was he, as a young rebel pilot many years ago, who destroyed the Empire's first orbital battle station, the Death Star. It was he who was trained by exiled Jedi Masters Obi-Wan Kenobi and Yoda to harness the powers of the Force, in hopes the boy might rise against me. And it was he who resisted my influence, turning his back on the dark side and the chance to rule the galaxy as my new apprentice. Skywalker would have been struck down for his insolence if not for the duplicitous actions of his father, Lord Vader. How fitting, then, that Skywalker would ultimately give his own life in battle against the child whose soul he failed to save—Ben Solo, the boy who had become Kylo Ren.

LEIA ORGANA

Luke Skywalker was not the only offspring of Lord Vader to stand against me. His twin sister, Leia Organa, was secreted away as an infant and raised as royalty on the planet Alderaan. She learned the art of diplomacy from her adopted father, a Republic traitor named Bail Organa. Those skills were wasted fostering a Rebel Alliance to oppose my rule. If Leia had proved to be as strong in the Force as her father and brother before her, perhaps I could have turned her to the dark side. But Lord Vader's betrayal ensured that would not come to pass. Instead, she chose a path far less rewarding. Yet, as a leader in the Resistance, Leia managed to become a constant thorn in the side of the First Order. Even with her brother dead and her son devoted to the dark side, the Princess of Alderaan continues to disrupt my plans. But her foolish acts will be in vain. Her will may be strong, but I have great experience bringing Skywalkers to heel.

KYLO REN

Young Ben Solo possessed what all masters live to see: raw, untamed power. But a great conflict raged within the boy as well. Not only did his inner turmoil make him heir apparent to his grandfather, Lord Vader, it also made him the perfect pawn. Using Snoke as my proxy, I reached into the boy's mind, influencing his choices. I turned him against the new Jedi Order that was rising in my absence. I severed his bonds to his family and broke his ties to the light. Once reborn as Kylo Ren, he was mine to control. From the shadows, I shaped him into a worthy apprentice—not a true Sith but equally powerful in the dark side. Rising to become a champion of the First Order, Kylo Ren helped spread fear in the galaxy once more. Yet, even after striking down Snoke and seizing control of the First Order, the boy remains conflicted. His Force connection to the girl, Rey—a bond I helped facilitate—has left him unbalanced. The final traces of light within him still struggle to regain control. I have given him one final test to prove his worth: Kill the girl, end the Jedi, and rule the galaxy. Even though he knows what must be done, I fear my young ally lacks the strength to do it . . .

THE RULE OF TWO

Vader was not my only apprentice. Nor was he the only one who failed me. Unlike the Jedi, who seemed willing to train practically any rabble who heard the whispers of the Force, Sith Lords were significantly more selective in their search for disciples. Though this was not always the case.

MASTER AND APPRENTICE

A millennium ago, the Sith and Jedi were nearly equal in number. But unchecked ambition and infighting turned our Order against itself. Weakened by their own hand, the Sith were nearly wiped from existence by the opportunistic Jedi. But there was a Sith Lord who survived the culling—the great Darth Bane. It was he who reshaped the Sith, creating a new hierarchy to ensure the survival of our Order. His Rule of Two dictated that only two Sith Lords could exist at any one time—a master to possess the unlimited power of the dark side and an apprentice to covet it. But no Sith is ever content merely coveting power. A true Sith takes that power for themselves. Lord Bane's own apprentice struck him down to claim Bane's place. And so began a magnificently vicious cycle. Many Sith apprentices—myself included—have supplanted their masters in order to ascend. Yet not all apprentices survive long enough to seize the power they were taught to desire . . .

DARTH MAUL

The son of Nightsister clan leader Mother Talzin, Maul was recruited as my apprentice at an early age. This fierce Zabrak warrior was meant to be my ultimate weapon against the Jedi. His journey into the darkness was cemented by a pilgrimage to Malachor, the site of a great Sith massacre. When Maul breathed in the ashes of his fallen Sith predecessors, he relived their terrible pain. His quest for vengeance against the Jedi was ignited. For many years, Darth Maul trained in secrecy. But as my plans for galactic dominance began to unfold, the time came to make his presence known. Maul struck fear into the hearts of the Jedi, but his threat would not last long enough. He was unceremoniously defeated by Obi-Wan Kenobi, cut in half and left for dead. Darth Maul's time as my apprentice ended in shame, but our paths would cross again. Through sheer force of will, Maul survived his dismemberment. He remade himself as the leader of a criminal syndicate, now fueled by personal vengeance against Jedi and Sith alike. He meddled in my affairs on countless occasions but never succeeded in obtaining the revenge he so desperately desired.

DARTH TYRANUS

With Darth Maul seemingly slain, I found myself in need of a new apprentice. While Maul had been groomed to become a Sith warrior from childhood, my next disciple walked the Jedi path for most of his long life. Born to royalty on the lush world of Serenno, Count Dooku was a political idealist who rightfully grew disillusioned with the Jedi and their Republic. He left the Order to return to a life of nobility on his homeworld. But the Force was not done with him yet. Knowing one as powerful and influential as he could be a valuable tool for the Sith, I seduced him to the dark side. Vowing to help me eradicate the corruption from the institutions he had once served, Dooku was reborn as Darth Tyranus. My new apprentice was instrumental in orchestrating my rise to the throne. It was he who led the Separatist threat, cementing my power within the Senate. And it was he who oversaw the creation of the clone army on Kamino. Lord Tyranus played his role well throughout the Clone Wars, spreading lies and mistrust while doing my bidding. But Dooku had schemes of his own, training secret apprentices in preparation for the day he would claim my power for himself. With betrayal on the horizon, his death—delivered at the hands of his replacement, Anakin Skywalker—would prove far more useful to me than his life.

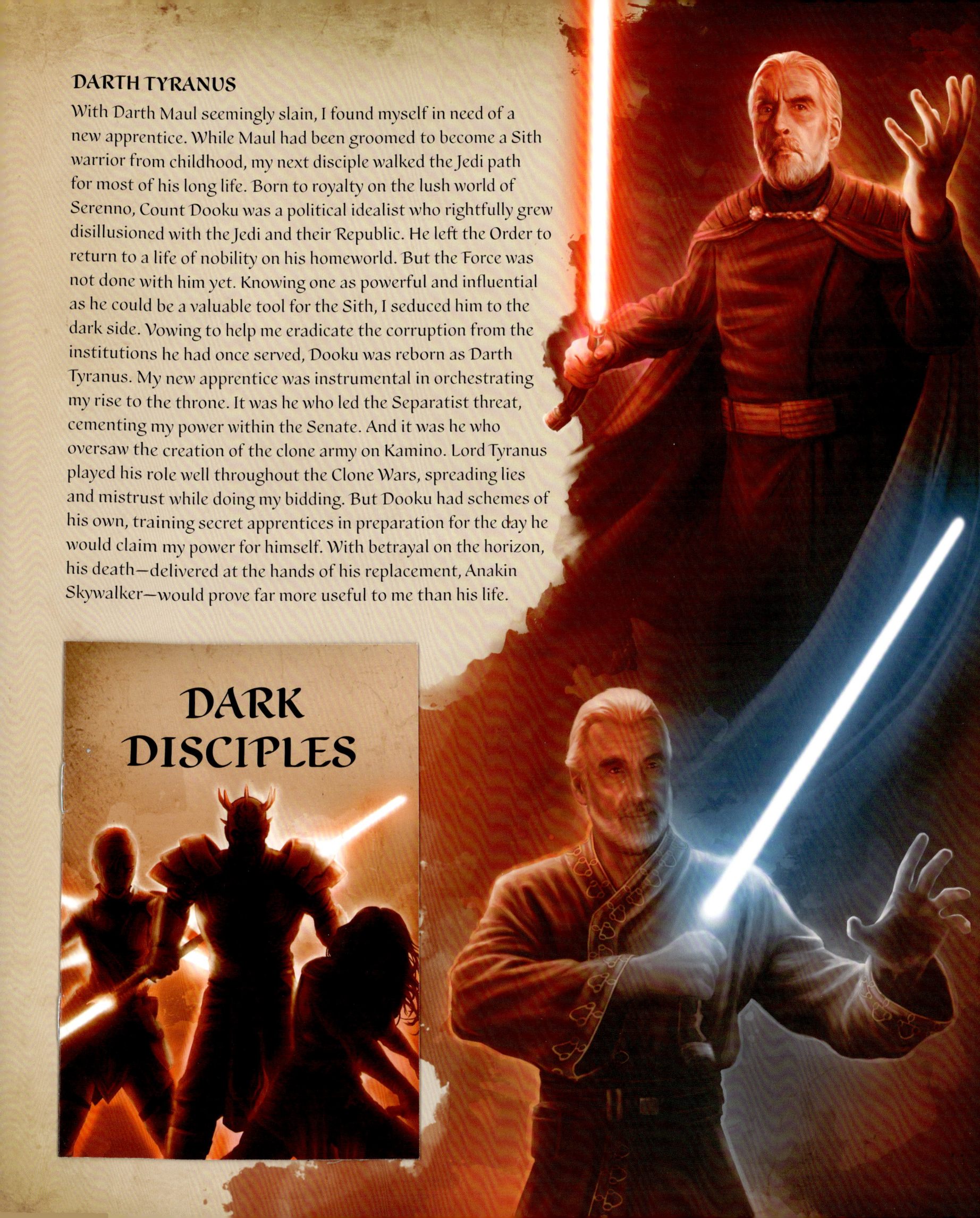

DARK DISCIPLES

LIGHTSABERS

To complement their mastery of the dark side, the Sith have long relied on an ancient, elegant weapon in combat: the lightsaber. The ignorant see the lightsaber as the shining symbol of the Jedi Knights. But it takes one truly adept in the ways of the dark side to wield a lightsaber as intended—with an unrestrained fury capable of delivering immeasurable harm.

DUEL TO THE DEATH

A lightsaber's plasma blade can cleave through virtually any substance, slicing through obstacles and dismembering opponents with ease. It can absorb and redirect powerful bursts of Force-generated lightning and deflect blasts from less sophisticated weaponry. The Jedi wield their lightsabers with caution and restraint, dulling the weapon's inherent lethal capabilities. But a Sith Lord subscribes to no such limitations. We embrace the full function of the lightsaber's design to deal untold suffering.

MAKE IT BLEED

The blade of the lightsaber brightly burns with energy, focused through the living kyber crystal within its hilt. Before the fall of their insipid Order, young Jedi would commune with the crystal they chose to place within their lightsaber, creating a balance between themselves and their weapon. Since kyber crystals are naturally attuned to the light side of the Force, those who serve the dark side must follow a different path. First, they must seize a pure crystal from the lightsaber of a Jedi they have vanquished in combat—for the saber of a Sith is not given. It is taken. Then, they must infuse that crystal with their pain, anger, and hatred, bending it to their will. This corrupts the crystal, aligning it with the dark side and making it bleed with unbridled crimson power. The bleeding process can yield unpredictable results. Some crystals shatter, making their energies unstable and unpredictable. Others resist their realignment, refusing to be bent toward the darkness. Once a crystal has been properly bled, the primal power it releases becomes not only a deadly instrument in the hands of a Sith Lord, but a symbol of their true strength in the dark side.

WARRIORS OF THE DARK SIDE

Few who devote themselves to the dark side of the Force ever prove worthy of being called Sith. But two Dark Lords alone, no matter how formidable, cannot conquer a galaxy. Over the years, I have strategically employed the service of lesser beings to advance my goals. In exchange for their loyalty, I have provided them power and influence in the galaxy far beyond what they could have achieved without my patronage.

THE INQUISITORIUS

The scant number of Jedi who managed to evade Order 66 fled to the far corners of the galaxy. To ensure the end of their legacy, I dispatched the Inquisitorius. These ruthless hunters were all former Jedi. Once slaves to the light, they were now awoken in service to the dark side. Under the watchful eye of Lord Vader, they would be sharpened into the blade that would sever the Jedi infection from the galaxy . . . at least for a time. Though fully expendable, the majority of my Inquisitors fulfilled their directive with great skill. They tracked down not only disgraced Jedi but any who might dare rekindle their fallen Order's flame. But as the number of surviving Jedi dwindled, I deemed the Inquisitorius obsolete . . .

NIGHTSISTERS & NIGHTBROTHERS

Dwelling in the fetid swamps of Dathomir, the Nightsisters were a coven of mystics who could tap into the dark energies of their planet with malicious effect. Long ago, I considered taking their leader, Mother Talzin, as my first apprentice. Forging a bond between my own dark powers and her arcane abilities seemed advantageous. But instead, I took something from Talzin that I considered far more valuable: her son Maul. The boy's vast potential would have been squandered had he remained on that abysmal planet as the witches kept their male counterparts, the Nightbrothers, subservient. I freed the boy from their servitude and brought him under my tutelage, an affront Talzin would never forgive. After Talzin and her kin made repeated attempts to eliminate my next apprentice, Darth Tyranus, no magic could save the Nightsisters from my unmitigated wrath.

THE ACOLYTES OF THE BEYOND

Not all who worship the dark side are strong with the Force. Some are merely fanatics who understand that the dark side is the one true path to victory—even if it is a path they are not capable of walking themselves. One such group of adherents was the Acolytes of the Beyond. They believed that the Force is akin to a river, and that the dark side is the only means of changing its currents. To alter the future in their favor, they devoted themselves to gathering Sith arcana, destroying the objects, and releasing the dark energies within as a sacrificial offering to the ancient Sith Lords. Later, the Acolytes wisely decided that these irreplaceable artifacts should be revered, not destroyed. Led by a number of extreme loyalists—including my former Imperial advisor, Yupe Tashu—the Acolytes relentlessly pursued Sith secrets, fueling their unwavering devotion to my cause.

THE KNIGHTS OF REN

Those who dwell in the Unknown Regions have long whispered legends of the Knights of Ren. This band of marauders was said to have burned their way across worlds, consuming everything in their path. In recent years, an enclave of warriors stepped from the darkness to claim that name—and the fear it instilled—as their own. Each of the Knights of Ren harbors the shadow of the dark side within them. But unlike the Sith, they are not trained to harness that connection to its fullest potential. The late Luke Skywalker once claimed that the Knights used the Force like a hammer rather than a blade—perhaps the only truth to ever fall from his lips. But for some jobs, a blunt instrument is more than sufficient. The Knights of Ren do not adhere to any code, doing whatever they must to triumph. The price to join their fabled ranks is simple: Choose a worthy target, and give them "a good death." This cost was one young Ben Solo paid in full when he struck down the group's master and assumed leadership of the Knights of Ren himself.

SITH ETERNAL

The galaxy has long trembled before the might of those who have sworn to execute my grand design. But the most committed of my followers have gone unseen, operating in secrecy here on Exegol. Seeking only my glory, the Sith Eternal have never wavered in their devotion. Their tireless works will soon be rewarded.

EXILED ON EXEGOL

While I ruled the Empire, few realized the full extent of my dark abilities. They witnessed my vast power yet were ignorant of how it had been gained. So as not to invoke irrational fears, I hid my true nature as a Dark Lord of the Sith. To avoid discovery, I divided my followers into factions. The Imperial fleet continued to enforce my will in the known galaxy. But the most devout of my acolytes, those invested in furthering my connection to the dark side, were relegated to the Unknown Regions. It was here, free from the prying eyes of rebels and Republics, that they—my loyal Sith Eternal—could fulfill the next step in my ascendancy.

THE FINAL ORDER

Unaware of my presence, far too many insignificant fools in the First Order attempted to seize power for themselves. For this galaxy to truly be mine once again, it would require total obedience from those beneath me. Such compliance could only come from those indoctrinated in the ways of the Sith from birth. My Sith Eternal would provide me the tools I needed. It was they who constructed a fully operational armada on Exegol at my command. It was they who trained their offspring to operate those vessels with deadly efficiency. For a generation, they toiled and trained, and now their efforts shall be put to the test as the Final Order prepares to arise!

SITH TROOPERS

The most elite members in my new army, these crimson soldiers are fully devoted to my noble cause. Far too often, clones and stormtroopers exhibited unseemly moments of free will. To eliminate such flaws, these fiercely loyal fighters have undergone extreme levels of mental conditioning and flash-imprinting. These processes have rendered them completely susceptible to my commands and have eliminated any chance of rebellion. Though they have come to be known as Sith troopers, these soldiers bear no connection to the Force. They are Sith in name only. But the brutality of their wrath may soon suggest otherwise.

THE OLD TONGUE

The most sacred of the prophecies studied by the Sith Eternal were transcribed in ur-Kittât, the forbidden language of the Sith. Like the dark side itself, ur-Kittât requires mastery to decipher. A simple change in inflection can alter a prophecy completely, opening ancient doctrines to a number of interpretations. The cowards of the Galactic Republic banned the language of the Sith in an attempt to bury its deep truths. Even protocol droids were prohibited from translating its hidden wisdom. Yet, just like the Order that spoke it, the Old Tongue refused to be erased. It still lives on in ancient Sith holocrons, on temple walls, and in the whispers of my most devoted disciples.

SITH FLEET

To assure my conquest of the known galaxy, thousands of next-generation Star Destroyers were assembled in the launch bays carved beneath the surface of Exegol. This Final Order has been equipped with superlasers capable of annihilating a planet from far orbit. Now, any who dare to challenge my rightful place in this galaxy will learn the same painful lesson as the scum on Jedha, Alderaan, and Hosnian Prime. None shall stand in the way of my return. The First Order was just the beginning. The Sith fleet will increase my forces ten-thousandfold.

SITH ARTIFACTS

When the ancient Sith were pushed toward annihilation, they left behind a legacy of lost artifacts scattered across the far reaches of the galaxy. Though my Final Order holds the key to the future of the Sith, these sacred relics have unlocked the history of our Order, providing great insight into the dark forces that empower us. Many of these revered objects proved indispensable as I laid the foundation for my triumphant return.

WAYFINDERS

Nearly impossible to navigate, the Unknown Regions contained hidden worlds where the ancient Sith could operate in secret. But so dangerous were these territories that even the Sith could not travel to them without proper guidance. To avoid certain death on their journeys, the Sith employed wayfinders. These ancient navigational tools identify safe pathways through even the most treacherous stretches of space. Only two wayfinders remain: one in the ruins of Vader's castle on Mustafar; the other locked in a vault on the wreckage of the second Death Star. Without these hyperspatial compasses, my refuge on Exegol remains undiscoverable.

HOLOCRONS

Some artifacts show the path to ancient secrets. But there are others that contain those great secrets themselves. A holocron is a holographic storage device, accessible only by one who is powerful in the ways of the Force. The Sith recorded their ancient teachings and lost knowledge of the dark side within these intricate apparatuses. Some holocrons were even said to be capable of housing the sentient presence of an ancient Sith Lord within them. Jedi holocrons were seen as prizes by those who desired an understanding of the Force, but I have scoured their Order's archives, and the so-called wisdom contained within is questionable at best. The Sith knew full well that knowledge is power, and power is not something to be shared. As such, a Sith holocron is a rare and extremely valuable object for any capable of unlocking the dark secrets inside.

RELICS

Pushing the Sith to the edge of oblivion was not enough for the Jedi. Their abhorrent Order defiled our most sacred shrines, burying them beneath their own temples in a rite of suppression and purification. But the secrets within those ancient sites would not remain buried. Sacred relics were still housed within their abandoned halls, waiting to be recovered. Over the years, I have sought out these forgotten temples, reclaiming their lost treasures in the name of the Sith. Ranging from ornate chalices and urns to power sources capable of widespread destruction, these remnants store dark energy that is as vital to the future of our Order as it was to its past.

Not all artifacts of the Sith were possessed by the Dark Lords themselves. Like any weapon used to cause immense suffering, the blades once wielded by Sith assassins resonate with the power of the dark side. Echoes of the pain delivered by these ancient implements can still be felt by those sensitive to the Force. Although they were forged to inflict agony, these weapons often served another purpose. Some were inscribed with ancient runes, pointing the way to lost Sith temples and forgotten treasures. These weapons have long been coveted, both for the power they contain and that which they might yet unleash.

SITH WORLDS

Exegol has become the new seat of Sith power as my worshippers prepare for the rise of the Final Order. But there are many other worlds still teeming with dark energy. Once we leave the Unknown Regions and spread our influence across the galaxy, we shall reclaim these worlds in the name of the Sith.

MORABAND

Known long ago as Korriban, this ancient homeworld of the Sith was abandoned after countless wars transformed it into an infertile wasteland. Although the world itself may be dead, the spirits of the fallen Sith entombed in the Valley of the Dark Lords live on eternally. As my power grows, I have heard the whispers of my predecessors calling to me from Moraband, offering me their dark secrets. When the time comes, I shall answer.

MALACHOR

Malachor is a lifeless planet remembered as the site of the Great Scourge—a battle that annihilated countless members of the Sith Order. Millennia ago, the vindictive Jedi ambushed the Sith on their own sacred ground. As the confrontation raged, an ancient superweapon within the Sith temple was activated. Not a single living thing on the planet survived. Only their petrified forms remained to tell their tale. Although the temple of Malachor has long since fallen, the pain of the massacred Sith still lives on, infused into the ashes that cover the barren world's surface.

DATHOMIR

I have spoken of the Nightsisters and Nightbrothers, members of the Zabrak race who made their home on Dathomir. The world they adopted is rich in the energies of the dark side, which they used to fuel their own mystical abilities. Dathomir is a dangerous world inhabited by a number of deadly creatures, such as the chirodactyl, an apex predator. But legends claim that the spirits of the slain Nightsisters still haunt the swamps of this wretched planet. Death by one of Dathomir's native beasts would be a merciful escape compared to the vengeful fury of those spiteful sorceresses.

MUSTAFAR

Beneath the sweltering surface of Mustafar's Gahenn Plains lies a powerful locus for the dark side of the Force. It was there, not far from the site of his greatest defeat, that Darth Vader built his fortress with the aid of Lord Momin—returned to life through the powers of his mask. The fortress's ebon spires were designed to tune the energies of this dark nexus. Lord Vader hoped to harness the planet's seething energies to break down the barrier between life and death. His efforts may have failed, but I believe that great secrets still lie beneath Mustafar's molten crust.

WORLD BETWEEN WORLDS

Beyond the known galaxy, beyond even the Unknown Regions, lies something far greater—the World Between Worlds. This mystical realm connects all of time and space, creating a conduit between the living and the dead. Those who control this plane would possess mastery over all of existence, but gaining access has proved an unexpected challenge. A gateway to the World Between Worlds was once opened in a lost temple on Lothal, but the portal was destroyed before I could seize the power within. Having touched this unusual realm for but a moment, I recognized the unfathomable potential it holds. Its power must be mine . . .

ILUM AND THE DEATH STARS

With a planetary core formed from kyber crystal, this small planet in the Unknown Regions was long held sacred to the Jedi. When their Order was eliminated, I dispatched my Imperial forces to extract Ilum's resources to fuel my Death Stars. With kyber-powered superlasers capable of obliterating planets, these orbital battle stations were meant to become the ultimate weapons in my Imperial arsenal. However, the design of the Death Stars proved to be fatally flawed, and much like Ilum before them, they would not last.

A DYAD IN THE FORCE

There are few secrets of the Force I have yet to master. But our Order's ancient prophecies speak of one fabled manifestation unseen for generations—a dyad. This pairing of two beings strong in the Force, linked together by an unbreakable bond, creates a power as strong as life itself.

TWO THAT ARE ONE

For a millennium, the Sith have adhered to the Rule of Two. But this decree is said to merely be a pale imitation of its predecessor, the Doctrine of the Dyad. Legends claim that two beings sharing this profound connection gain access to a great number of abilities—skills beyond the grasp of even the most powerful Force wielder. Members of a dyad were believed to be capable of transferring their life force to heal others. Some could even pass physical objects through time and space in an instant. If two Sith were bonded so deeply as to transcend their physical beings, the power they could unlock together would know no limits.

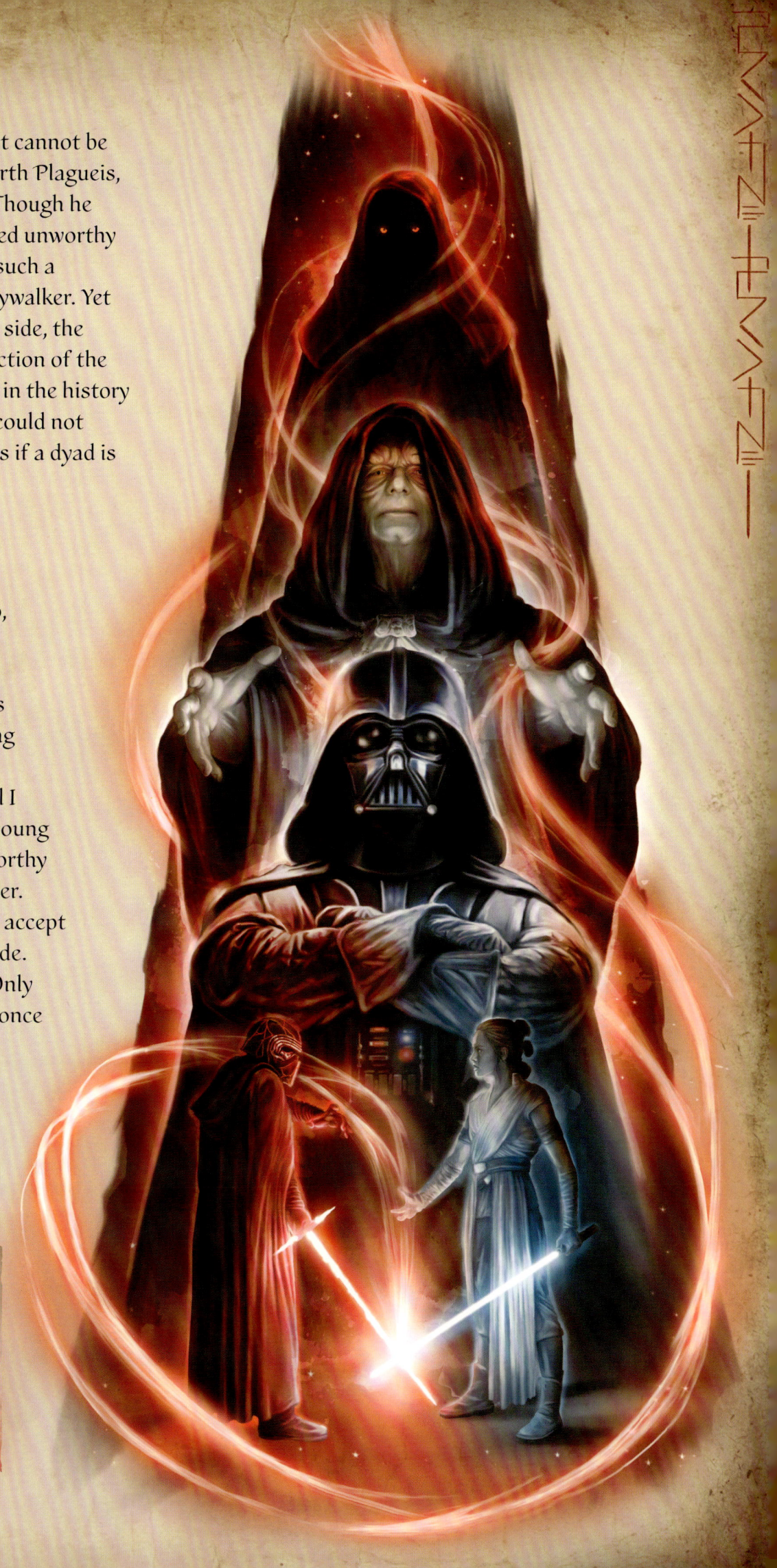

BROKEN BONDS

The dyad is an elusive connection, one that cannot be created through will alone. My master, Darth Plagueis, attempted to forge such a bond with me. Though he was wise in the ways of the Force, he proved unworthy of the task. I, too, attempted to facilitate such a connection with my apprentice Anakin Skywalker. Yet even with the so-called Chosen One at my side, the balance we shared paled against the perfection of the dyad. If the two most powerful bloodlines in the history of the galaxy—Palpatine and Skywalker—could not produce such a bond, the question remains if a dyad is possible at all.

FORGING THE FUTURE

The Doctrine of the Dyad was etched into the walls of my citadel on Exegol eons ago, a constant reminder of its significance to our Order. To my Sith Eternal, the dyad is not merely the stuff of ancient legend; it is the future of the Sith—the key to unlocking the full potential of the dark side. But if a new dyad is to be formed, with whom shall I share its legendary power? It is doubtful young Kylo Ren will ever prove himself a more worthy apprentice than his grandfather, Lord Vader. Perhaps, then, my lost granddaughter will accept her birthright and rule the galaxy by my side. My visions have not yet made that clear. Only one thing is certain: When a dyad returns once more, it shall usher in the dawn of a new era. And I will be there to claim its power in the name of the Sith.

> DZWOROKKA YUN;
> NYÂSHQÙWAI, NWIQÙWAI.
> WOTOK TSAWAKMIDWANOTTOI,
> YUNTOK HYARUTMIDWANOTTOI

CONCLUSION

And so the Sith rise again!

   Long have I awaited this day. Already, a wave of terror washes across the galaxy as the specter of my presence looms. Even those who once lived under the yoke of the Empire know not what awaits them upon my return.

   My Final Order is prepared to take flight. The time has come to remind the galaxy of the true power of the Sith. Planets will fall. Billions will cry out in pain, only to be silenced. But when the smoke clears, those who still stand will swear their loyalty to me—for they will have no other choice.

   Some will oppose my efforts. But with Luke Skywalker's threat removed, few remain who possess the power to challenge my supremacy. Leia Organa's pathetic Resistance has been decimated by the First Order. None have dared to answer their desperate pleas for help. And Kylo Ren is too torn between the dark and the light to pose a threat to my reign. The menace of the Skywalker bloodline is no longer a concern.

   Only the scavenger, Rey, exhibits the potential to prove my equal in the Force. I must bring her home so that she may claim her inheritance and her rightful place among the Sith. Yet I am well aware that even with such great hatred flowing through her, young Rey will not be turned to the dark side easily. The poor, deluded girl imagines herself the last of the Jedi, after all. And thus, the destruction of the Sith remains her ultimate goal.

   But this child of my own blood will not be the end of our Order. She shall be a new beginning! For when she seeks her vengeance and strikes me down, it is I who shall prevail. There is no vessel in the galaxy more worthy of my infinite might than a child of my own flesh. With a slash of her lightsaber, my spirit will pass into her. We two will be reborn as one . . .

   . . . and once more, the Sith will rule the galaxy. Eternally.

TITAN BOOKS

A division of Titan Publishing Group Ltd
144 Southwark Street
London SE1 0UP
www.titanbooks.com

Find us on Facebook: www.facebook.com/TitanBooks
Follow us on Twitter: @TitanBooks

© & ™ 2021 LUCASFILM LTD. Used Under Authorization.

Published by Titan Books, London, in 2021.

No part of this book may be reproduced, stored in a retrieval system, or transmitted, in any form or by any means without the prior written permission of the publisher, nor be otherwise circulated in any form of binding or cover other than that in which it is published and without a similar condition being imposed on the subsequent purchaser.

A CIP catalogue record for this title is available from the British Library.
ISBN: 978-1-78909-941-6

Published by arrangement with Insight Editions, PO Box 3088, San Rafael, CA 94912, USA. www.insighteditions.com

Publisher: Raoul Goff
VP of Licensing and Partnerships: Vanessa Lopez
VP of Creative: Chrissy Kwasnik
VP of Manufacturing: Alix Nicholaeff
Editorial Director: Vicki Jaeger
Art Director: Stuart Smith
Executive Editor: Chris Prince
Editorial Assistant: Harrison Tunggal
Managing Editor: Lauren LePera
Senior Production Editor: Elaine Ou
Senior Production Manager: Greg Steffen
Senior Production Manager, Subsidiary Rights: Lina s Palma

FOR LUCASFILM
Senior Editor: Brett Rector
Creative Director of Publishing: Michael Siglain
Art Director: Troy Alders
Story Group: Leland Chee and Emily Shkoukani
Lucasfilm Art Department: Phil Szostak
Lucasfilm Asset Management: Sarah Williams, Erik Sanchez, Bryce Pinkos, Chris Argyropoulos, and Gabrielle Levenson

Illustrations by Sergio Gómez Silván

Insight Editions, in association with Roots of Peace, will plant two trees for each tree used in the manufacturing of this book. Roots of Peace is an internationally renowned humanitarian organization dedicated to eradicating land mines worldwide and converting war-torn lands into productive farms and wildlife habitats. Roots of Peace will plant two million fruit and nut trees in Afghanistan and provide farmers there with the skills and support necessary for sustainable land use.

Manufactured in China by Insight Editions

10 9 8 7 6 5 4 3 2 1